BACK OF MOUNT PEACE

POEMS

KWAME DAWES

PEEPAL TREE

First published in Great Britain in 2010
Peepal Tree Press Ltd
17 King's Avenue
Leeds LS6 1QS
UK

ISBN 13:9781845231248

Supported by
**ARTS COUNCIL
ENGLAND**

CONTENTS

For Kojo, Aba, Adjoa, Gwyneth, Kojovi
for
Mama the Great
for Sena, Kekeli and Akua
and for
Lorna for being there always.
Remembering Neville

Note
These poems owe much to the colour, imagery and spiritual grace of the paintings of South Carolina Low Country artist, Jonathan Green.

PROLOGUE

DREAM

This poem arrives as a poem but broken. It comes
in images without the energy to make itself

into a plot, it sulks by the wayside. Dumb
poem, it pontificates about living on the shelf,

about how much it is underrated; about how a poem
is art free of the ransoming of Mammon.

This poem does not know where it began,
does not have a path to a tragedy

as complex as love and its details, the way
a song can become a life lived. This poem

is, after all, something I probably could not say
awake, scared of finding out what it means.

So I write out the poem, the repeating metaphor
never sure of itself, always hungry for more.

ONE

Found

FOUND

She did not know her name standing on the hook
of the road to Brown's Town where the chattering ghosts
of forty market women hover. The way she shook,
it was as if she saw them, felt them post
their revelations in her head.

                        She did not know
her name, this round body, orange in the dew,
when I came upon her.
                  She was naked, her breasts
low with weight not age, her eyes almost blue,
the negro of her settled in her hips and the curl
of her pubic hair. She shivered on the crest
of the hill, no clues to her life except the thin
line on her wedding finger, a butterfly tattoo
on her sloping shoulder, and the flame-red sheen
of nail polish on her toes.
                I asked her who
she was; she said nothing, then repeated, *Who?*

So I named her Esther, and her eyes flew
away from me, high into the sullen sky;
then she sang a hymn that made the pea doves fly.

SPARROW

His army fatigues shirt swallows
the dull yellow of her body,
turning her into a shivering sparrow
stranded wingless at an oak tree's

root; flight is a forgotten dream.
He gathers her and leads her,
dumb child, down to the stream
where he washes her with care.

The streaks of blood, the twigs
caught in the entanglement
of her hair, now a matted wig –
the tarnished vestment

of a woman who has abandoned
beauty and decorum for rest.
She lets herself be his burden
as he holds her to his chest.

SIN

Beneath the embossment of clouds,
inside the frame of winded sheets,

lies the sea, muddy green with its infested shroud
of sargasso. Esther stands in straw hat and pleats,

gazing into the new day, her head
cleansed of memories, her eyes set

like the constant stare of the dead
who are incapable of staunching the regrets

and sorrows they have caused. She
is, though, a prophecy in my heart

and I confess a sinner's hunger
for her full globe breasts and parts

that shimmer with salty sorrows.
Pray, Lord, give me holier tomorrows.

TOMATOES

Where women fry figs in fat-back
and season their hominy grits with ground pepper,
deep in their polka-dotted, quilt-walled shacks,
where a grinning child can cure amnesia,
Esther stews tomatoes, red and plump,
in vinegar with thyme and garlic cloves.

Everything smells of greeting and welcome,
of mother's love, the surprise of flown doves.

And here where God pours mercy over blanched days,
spreading it like a miracle over green cotton fields,
I pray that the pickled grace of tomato paste
will soak my balls and cleanse my seed
of the canker of bad love, the rot of old sin,
so that the hallelujahs of new love may begin.

WOMAN SMELL

A week later, her smell slips
under his door, moves softly
through the room, drips
syrup on his face slowly

while he sleeps at night:
the scent of the sea, or something
old and full of the bright
taste of fresh blood. It lingers

around the gloomy pantry,
then rises as a memory: the aroma
he remembers in the galley
where Loretta rode out

contractions, and spilt a universe
of shit, blood, water, sweat;
that ground smell of new birth;
the smell that stirs now in his chest.

THE HABITS OF LOVE

Since his wife Loretta's death, Monty collects
the burn-stained clicking carcasses of bulbs,
storing them in cotton stuffed into plastic
pastel-coloured party cups. He shelves

them in the tinder box-shed in the back yard
visiting them each week as a ritual
for the dead. He tries not to discard
the multiples, but relishes the collapsed oval

of one he found glowing in an open field,
the sun humming in the shattered filament,
as if the earth fed power to make light bleed
through, so a man would stare in wonderment.

It is still the cherished one, despite the hundreds
he has gathered in the gloomy innards
of his shed. Esther has seen but not said
a thing; so grand his pain, so hard, so hard.

MERCY

From the house, Monty sees how dust
from the ploughed earth covers a blue
sky; gloom is written on the rusted
surface of the day, and the news

comes from the city: how thousands
have been slaughtered by planes
hurtling into the stoic stand
of buildings – and he explains

to his dog that each day gifts
are wrenched from us; that death
by bloody hands is how God sifts
us, breaks us. He gives us births

bloody and miraculous to show
his mercies; but we must kneel in the dust
and pray for good fortune – like how to know
a woman's love and how to taste her lust.

BAPTISM I

A valley of red poppies stretches to the forest's edge
above which a sky of fragile blue, wide open,

stares down. Vi, Liz and Pet, the carriers of knowledge,
stand sentinel with their open sheets of white – plain

protection for Esther who is naked but for a bandana.
They bathe her in a steaming pan of mint leaves,

the calming caress of ginger, and the air is tempered
by the aroma of boiled irises. This is the ritual of grief.

She must prepare before the journey –
wingless and earth-rooted – that she must make.

Such a long way from the milk and honey
of the cloudy rest where sweet hallelujahs break.

I watch her emerge, new name, new mission,
and all is soiled by my unholy fascination.

THE IDEA OF HER

For days he bears an unending fatigue with him,
avoiding sleep at night to escape the idea of her,

to avoid turning on his belly to grind
out the persistent longing. He wakes on the hour,

stares at the low glow of dogwood blossoms,
sips water to slake his gravelled throat. In the day,

he walks in dreams, her sweat in his nose, the dumb
circle of fog blunting any strength to turn away

the feel of her. She is in his skin, settled in him,
though he cannot speak it. He catches the scent

of passing women. His eyes assess the curve and trim
of their backsides. He compares, then resents

these futile infidelities – their impotence.
He can smell her in the air, a clinging fragrance.

COLOURED CLOTHES

Someone cuts strips of navy-blue dotted cloth
and spreads them across the sky. The wind

blows everything – the fluid swirl, a broth
of unsettled leaves. The mother bends

to gather the wrung-damp clothes her baby
hands up to her. It is Saturday, washday

and this quilted tapestry is turning me
to prayer. I am searching for the easy way

of faith, and the music of a goddess
standing in the deep blue light with her

industry – a proverb for wealth. The rest
is the requiem that the living will hear

when God thunders from the belly of faith,
when we all tremble at his fire and wrath.

STEAMED FISH SUPPER

She eats the steamed snapper with practised efficiency
like my mother. She casually sucks in whole parts
then, staring ahead, her mouth moves, familiarly.

Suddenly, thin white bones make a surreal art
of her lips. They hang there bobbing. She gathers them
into a cupped palm as she swallows the flesh;

her mouth, pink and tender, can now open
for more fish. She knows how she likes it, fresh
and liquid with coconut milk, the bammy steamed

and gummy in the okra slime. Esther does this as if she has
lived in a village where women interrupt their dreams
with the hope of their men returning with bass,

tuna, shark, and pink snapper.
                              I eat in fear,
praying, hoping she does not remember.

ADAPTATION

I am growing
another chamber

to hold
this woman

in my heart
    without breaking it.

FISHERMAN

The retired fisherman now builds houses, contracts
for labour. It's not like fishing when you had to dip
your fingers into blood, had to risk the cataracts

and the dumb silence of the wide river and that slip
of cloud over on the otherwise unchanging sea and sky.

Then, a man felt the salt of his sweat, and smelt
the wretched stench of his own shit; then he'd cry
through the night at the memory of his mother's welts,
the long finger marks of her man's open palm.

Now, he is retired to Esther and her blank slate,
an empty page of textured off-white sheets, the calm
surface on which he will write of desire and hate.

Sometimes a tender infant fish is too lovely
to toss back into a yawning, craven sea.

PEACH PICKING

From the dusty road under acacia trees
the house looks like a dream rising in sharp
colours from the common green, passive sea

of unremarkable land. Esther lifts the tarp
and gathers gently the bruised peaches, their water
puckering the skin like a blister, the childishness

of their tender peel — how little it takes to mark
them. She fills baskets, planting fruit in a nest
of fresh damp straw, while she counts out

a song that turns into words; a song that feels
as old as the indigo sky and the stoic brick house

in the middle of nowhere; a body with no context,
just the language of loss, haunting as a low country hex.

IN THE BONE

The doctor reads my bones; they are clues of a history
set in greys, whites and consuming blacks.

He draws closer, touching the tailbone sharply
turned down. *What beatings!* he says. *Your back
broken maybe by falls; you jumped much, falling
hard, but your body's supple enough to forget. There
on the hip, a chip of calcium floats, a wounding,
maybe, something sudden*, but I feel no searing
pain in my hip. It moves with fluid ease.

It is my spine, between the wings of my back,
that has crippled me. The hip is free
of fusing; it is normal. Yet how he talks:

*Your pelvis, so small, yet opened out enough
for a child's head. Oh, you suffered*, he laughs.

AGE

Do I count the lines turning up
towards the raisin mole on my temple,
measure the depth of that soft cup
where my neck meets the ample

heft of my breasts? Should I trace
the pattern of veins on my hands
or the spindle of wrinkles on my face
to calculate the sum of my age?

Impossible to arrive at a simple number,
so I stack up the estimations
of those who let me pester
them with uncomplicated division.

I arrive at the pure average of my days:
I am giddy as a stumbling toddler,
two-headed as a teen gone astray,
war-seasoned as a grey-haired elder.

PELVIS

It is enough to turn her from the glaring light,
to stare out into the grey and bright colours

of the parking lot; the jigsaw of her splintered sight,
drawing her away from the naked tremor

in her bones. The doctor still chuckles, *Maybe three,
could be four, children; the wear and tear, all natural.*

*A miracle, such low small hips, like a tree
low swung, too close to the ground, a veritable*

anomaly! She feels the heavy swell of her womb;
the contracting of every muscle in her belly,

and then the rest is shadows – a world long gone.
It is not easy to explain the tears, the misery

in her eyes, so she whispers, *Dead, dead, everyone
gone; they came and left, everyone, everyone gone.*

WHITE BREAKERS

Esther sprints across the open beach,
her voice a contralto to the child's
squeal and yell, trying to reach
above the foamy waves' wild

white breakers. She moves
with a mountain girl's agile
grace, and children sprint in droves
around her, the air fragile

with the uncertain memory
of what she has left behind,
the way she grows weary
with wondering. Lucinda,

a girl with locks like black grapes,
holds her face and says,
You have my mother' shape
but my sister's ways.
Amen.

THE BODY

The body, though, does not forget its grievances,
its complaints, the mouldy tiny toenail; the triggering

thumbs with the dark brown lines where incisions
were made; the stomach's violence each morning;

the bitter dryness at the back of the throat: the body
is a map of old ailments and compensations become

permanent. I trace a finger along the scar's steady
curve beneath my left breast, a mark of some

terrible fear, some hidden thing. I touch the breast
trying to calculate what terror, what lamenting

must have taken me at the news. The rest
are phantoms, for though the body knows, forgetting

is easier, and I know it is the fear of cataclysm
that makes me welcome this blankness, this chasm.

EVIDENCE

She traces with her finger the amber
lines emanating from her navel –
the story of how a body builds layers
of fat to cushion the head of a child

growing in the salt waters swirling
in her. These lines are remnants
of the glorious dome, the swelling
before the release through the crescent

scar under her belly – a keloid
rise that she fingers, a comforting
ritual while she waits at night for the void
of deep sleep. These, plus the evidence

of hard thickening skin just below
her vagina, where the rip of birth
healed into a still tender furrow
of skin, are the brandings of a mother.

PIANO

My fingers spread, tighten, understand
the pressure and give; a language
crawling up from deep, deep down;
each chord or note a response to the baggage

of meaningless prompts. But they form
reason, the melody of grace.
I play the piano with dumb
assurance, thoughtlessly racing

over keys, hardly surprised
by the sound that leaps out.
My eyes are closed and nothing arrives
but the knowledge of the next note.

On the walk in pitch darkness
home from the church, my heart
races. I am afraid of the universe
of memory buried in my new-found art.

ANOMIE

Esther's skin takes to the sun well.
                           On days
when the sun smashes into her unflinching stare
as she searches the sea for the hint of grey
against the startling cove's sheer
sheets crimpled under light, she turns
dark as mahogany – a mellow crawling
of Africa over her skin; and she lets the burns
heal under copious palms-full of butter, greasing
every part of her to a slick smoothness.
                                  She lets
me map her story along the stretch marks, patterns
of tenderness.

                Esther sings hymns into the gloom
and when she does I see her return
to some lost love, a memory, a child, a room
of her belonging.

                I have stopped searching the papers,
listening to the news, wishing she will remember.

BAPTISM II

Come morning, I leave the cool sand of the beach
and, before sun, I cross the wet tarmac

of the coastal road, and feel the soft sod and grass reach
to caress my feet, wet as the air here in the back

of this land, down where all the heavy histories
have settled into a thick morass, down here where

mushrooms rot the earth to life under the crowding trees,
the way shadow and green are sparked by the rare

blood-red poison of these wild azaleas. Back here
in the deep potbelly of the land, I find three women

waiting: the white sheet, a shelter; the pewter
basin filled with steaming mint and ginger stems.

I strip to my first self, pimples rising on my breasts.
Then slowly I am baptized in the blues' holy rest.

TWO

A Woman Wants

Now Boaz said to her at mealtime, "Come here, and eat of the bread, and dip your piece of bread in the vinegar." So she sat beside the reapers, and he passed parched grain to her; and she ate and was satisfied, and kept some back.

Ruth 2:14

COLOUR

The world should always be robust with colour –
a surfeit of palettes, the world an artist makes
when at dawn he wakes suddenly with the fever
to go to the canvas, to stand before it and let break
from his head every colour he has dreamt:

the streak of lemony gold on a bandana, the glints
of the women's ear loops, the lavender and mint
green of that woman's apron, the indigo spilling
on the pin-striped nurse's blouse, that orange
– no pure tube paint, something holier –
of her sister's scarf, and the patchy brown
and vanilla soft of a woman's naked shoulders.

Here white is a statement, the mystery of concealing
the precious soft centre and a saint's revealing.

ESTHER IN SHEER STOCKINGS

Esther wears green the colour of collards
and the pleats fan out above her black tights.

I touch the pew's wood for something hard
to keep me from reaching to caress the bright
glow of her skin under those sheer black stockings.

Flesh is the canker of these deaconesses
who come to sing hymns on new Sundays
in their silk and satin, cling-tight dresses

and their hats flamboyant – such a display
that makes a man's prayers a pitched battle

in the sanctuary! The world is wet from the heat
in the church today, and I start to buckle
at the shouts of glory and the beat

of a tambourine's golden arc of light,
turning me into old David itching for a fight.

BLOOD

I am surprised by the heaviness in my ankles
and the ballooning in my middle, by the flow
of water from me – my tears smoothing the wrinkles

in my skin; by the full and constant glow
of desire in my womb before the blood arrives
late at night. In half sleep I stumble

to the toilet and search, as if I will discover
the women's paraphernalia I need dumped
in the cupboard under the sink. But I only recover

a worn cotton cloth which I fold and tuck
under me after a long bath and weeping.
Somewhere, I keep recalling the dust,

the screaming children, the stomach's cramping
from fear or shame: the child again turning woman.

DREAM WORDS

When she talks in her sleep, he comes close, stoops
over her to listen. She is naked and words spill
out, like the sudden revelation when a swoop

of wind that morning bared her muddy nipples
and the dark triangle between her thighs, leaving her
vulnerable on the beach. He sips her soft

muttering, her lips making words: "Musgrave", "porcelain",
"mortar", "plaster of Paris," "fortissimo," "doves".
They bubble up from a dark green pond of sounds

he cannot decipher. The words arrive
fully formed, sweet round words on her tongue,
the country accent swallowed by an alien sound alive

in her mouth. He is shaken by the fearfulness of it all;
the universe in the secret pink memories she recalls.

REGENERATION

After his wife, the one who mothered
each dropped seed sprouting wild
on the hillsides, then fathered
those that came, eyes opened wide

and wailing from her vagina;
after she bore the shame of his
mannish disregard – a reminder
that in this island man's bliss

is a patient woman's pain;
after she could take no more
and died dumbly in the rose garden,
he buried her then closed the door

to all women, his unspent seed
spilling out in dreams until that, too,
dried up. Now a dead forgotten need
has awakened in him, all torn and new.

RELAPSE

1

Some
disease

linger-
linger

till one hearty day

it turn
your whole world
'round

2

Her mouth
smarts
and waters

Before the burst
of light

fills her throat

she knows
she knew.

A WOMAN WANTS

She wants a man who can turn his nose to smell rain
before the clouds have come; a man who waits patiently
in open fields for the deluge to soak through his skin.

A man who places his cheeks on her round belly
whispering messages, listening for it to say, *Plant the hoe*
now, while I still carry moisture, just below the cracked

skin of my belly. A man sweats into the land, a slow
labourer whose toes sink deep into soil. He will fall back
to the ground knowing she will cradle him, suck him

down deeply, letting his roots curl around sod and feed
from her constant streams. She wants a man whose eyes brim
with tears at the sight of the first shoots breaking the seed's

shell. This man will know when to be just a breath
and when she longs to inter him in her soft earth.

CHIVALRY
Ruth 3:7

There is always the art of making deals as if they are not
deals. So I lie at his feet, his soles rest on my belly,
feeling my warmth crawling up his legs to his crotch.

I sense him stir, look at me and wonder should he
take me now, read me as a careless, easy fuck, or should
he let his light catch my eye, see I have holier uses.

He is a soft man, a good man and I have understood
him better than he knows himself in the moment he rises,
ashamed at his erection, startled by my warm passivity.

He will do the right thing: first for decorum and grace
and then for the hunger – his lust, whet with mysteries
I give, a slow burn of a bush fire below the surface.

He thinks he's noble, so this must be a calculated dance;
it will never happen if all is left to chance.

THIS MAN SHOULD

This man should search the city, not for his lover
but for the man who owns her, the man who holds
her by the binding contracts of writs and lawyers.

A less pessimistic man would ignore it all, cuckold
the fool and count his pleasures daily. He has the power
of the present and her gratitude will trump all laws
of decency. She will come to him at night and shower
him with kisses and tears. But this man knows the raw
canker of things left to chance and he loves her too much
to risk the consuming enslavement she wakes in him.

To suddenly lose it all, to stand by and watch
another man take her back would be death to him.

He should search the city for the man, offer money
as payment for the blessings of serendipity.

AFTER THE PARTY

In deep sleep, her open mouth breathes
the musky fermentation of a bellyful of wine;
her nakedness strewn across the sheets.
He lies awake, remembering the shine

of her drunken abandon, the laughter,
the tears, her body's gyrations
finding muscles in her stomach like water
rolling over rocks – another woman.

Beside her now, he whispers a story
of abandonment, of cruel lovers,
of dead babies, of a tragic history,
hoping to seed in her unguarded ears

a memory that will tie her down,
make her cling to him. His crying
frightens him, how she has broken
in him every hard and sure thing.

SWING

Esther's laughter is shot with fear
as she pushes her legs forward
to carry her body into the gaping air.
Then bending knees to swing backward

blindly into the loop of the pendulum,
her stomach flips, her hands
clutch the rusty chain-links,
and each swoop rotates the land.

The void sucks her into sky,
her heart thrumming for the sweet
thoughtless release of flight,
her body chasing her feet.

It is here again, that familiar
elation and despair – the things
she fears when Monty fingers
the heat of her under-skin.

LOVING

Your foot
tuck inside

my armpit –
slick now

with my sweat
and you giggle

and you wriggle
and you giggle

and you wriggle.

EMBRACE

A body's shape changes. I feel it softening
against me like the welcome comfort of a warm

room after the chill outside. So I loosen
for an instant my protection from the sudden storm

of blood and desire, and grow tender,
finding carnal solace in a memory. It feels

like when I prayed for Christ to wipe the tears
from the broken face of my dead wife. So I heal

in the body, gathering in and keeping close
the thirst for love and the hunger

for sinful comforts. But the need in me grows.
Look at how I try to read lust in the way her

knees give way to my thighs, the way all sound
is swallowed by this soft thunder in the ground.

PINK SNAPPER

The pink snapper lies dumbly on the teak board;
the green light from the window creates a mosaic
of rainbow light, like the jewel of petrol spread
on rain water; the eyes and the thick pathetic
lips gleam with life. This is before the bitch-knife
chops the scallions, the fat tomatoes, the onions,
then crushes garlic, cilantro and thyme; before her brief
work on the ripe pineapple; before the warm oven
and the aroma of seasoned flesh baking, caramelizing
the raw pink tenderness into a savoury confection.

Esther cooks with the intensity of a daring
lover who has waited chastely for the return
of her man.
            And when he tastes the pepper and tamarind,
her body shudders, a plague of tiny bumps on her skin.

SOUP

Before the storm that called her out into its chaos
deep in August, a night so dark our fingers vanished
as they groped their way through trees, I understood loss

by accepting for the first time the pleasure, the relish
of her laughter, which came in waves above the silky
vapours rising from the deep porcelain bowl full

of a soup of pink crab-flesh, long slips of celery,
with carrots, beans and watercress tangled and pulled
down by soft tendrils of rice noodles. This light

pond sparkled on the surface with the hint of oil
and lily pads of steamed lettuces. I asked all night
what secret thing she had slipped in – to set to boil

my blood, my desire, my laughter, my abandon,
but she just pursed her lips as her brazen eyes shone.

THRILL BUMPS

The way
you call

my name

and make
a rash

of thrill bumps
burn my skin

is murder to me.

AT THE FAIR

From a distance at the fair, Esther does not seem
like someone I have carried on the hill roads twisting
sharply like the jagged polygraph lines of my dreams

to this place of balloons and white faces looking
like the mummified gaze of American gothic children
singing glee-club ballads with little joy and great

boredom. From afar she seems alone, her dark skin
against the white light of summer. I wait
for her eyes to tear before I come forward to hold

her hand and calm their jumping darting from
face to sudden sound, as if looking for her old
self in a memory. Last night's coupling

was a strain, until she made my sex rise
when she said, *Man, you is man,* in that tiny voice.

FULL-UP

If you bury me
in the wet

tonight

I will laugh

the way my heart
full-up wid you.

BUTTERFLY

There is an itch under her skin
where the indigo butterfly
has settled on the smooth sheen
of her shoulder. She tries

to stop the fluttering, her nail
pressing in. The pain is a ghostly
remembrance of the needle
stabbing in coloured bursts, quickly.

I place a damp mouth there,
my tongue caressing as if
to wipe away the mere
hint of another man's gift

and brand of ownership.
I suck hard till she cries.
Then I pull away my lips
from the obscene butterfly.

THREE

The Things She Knows

Then she said, "I have found favour in your eyes, my lord, for you have comforted me and spoken kindly to your servant, though I am not one of your servants."

Ruth 2:13

BEAUTIFUL

I have danced
to sweat
and forgetting

I am beautiful

I dance
my hips heavy
with language

I am beautiful

SEA

Today she stares out to sea, moving her lips
as if she is reading her past in the undulation
of waves, and he watches her, fearful that this will trip
something in her, take her back to the commotion
of her history.
              The sun rests on her. The sea turns red,
then indigo, that deep purple before the black;
and she stares out, silent, waiting.
                        Once, she said
that if it all came back she would lie, pretend the track
back to herself was never there, just so he would
understand that he was her happiness. That promise
seems lost now, with her eyes trying to read
into something on the open sheet of sea, her shoulders
defiant; a back with no assurances, just the dread
reminder that those pleasures, those sweet days are dead.

DELTA

There is a place where the fresh waters
travelling down mountains,
cutting through valleys, arrive
at the salt of the ocean. Water

sighs at this meeting and nothing
is settled here, a constant unknowable
self: beyond the delta is the sea
yawning, consuming. Behind,

the assurance of river banks,
a charted, reliable journey.
Esther stands at the river's mouth,
feeling the cool of its flow

against her back with the warm
suck of salt sea on her belly.
To swim out is to meet meaning,
memory and fear. She drifts backwards.

SILENCES

My silence sulks like a gorgon squatting
in the corner of the room — one of the ignored
ones — everything about me quickly becoming
mute faced. These days, I know I am more
inscrutable than those months when my dumb
silences were the failure of language.

Now I hoard words, wearing my gloom
with calculation. I will gauge
his love by his efforts to clear the bellicose
air. I wait without regret, as if
I have arrived at the new calculus
of long-suffering love.

                I will him to lift
my skirt, plant his lips on my brown belly
and whisper light into my flesh, tenderly.

WAKING FROM SLEEP

On dark nights
I wake to voices
crawling over me

Sometimes
the rain
whispers my name

Sometimes
I find God
leaving me

Sometimes
I cup my breasts
and feel their milk

BLACK SAND

Dawn falls lightly on the black sand beach.
The air here is heavy with the wet of the sea.

The coconut fronds, green and edged yellow, reach
out to the grey sky. A kind light, misty

and soft, gathers around everything. At six,
the sun is delayed and a woman, yellow

skinned and glowing, holds a crooked stick
out over the water as if she's trying to let flow

something from hand to restless waves. She is
standing in the black sand; it sucks her feet

deeper. She knows she is starting to miss
the swollenness of mothers. She fears the heat

and the cravings
                that keep crawling
                              beneath her skin.

AGAINST FREE WILL

A grand plan: everything meets, collides, and forms
within the architecture of a man and his God
who does not let him steal much, though in storms
Monty has sometimes heard the melody of His rod.

And he has taken this to be an allowance – a gift
for his dreams. There is, though, order in the patterns
he finds in himself. His manner is slow and he shifts
into the proper slots only when the voice returns
with news of dry ground, olive trees and a place
he can stand on, safe from the flood waters.

Perhaps, he thinks, he should be the bird, or the stitcher of lace,
the one who obeys simple instructions. Better
to be the sent one, the one with the news of promise
than to be some bewildered seeker of fleece.

SEER

Last night
you look

at me hard
then soft

like you see
something

old and sad
in me.

MEMORY

Only sometimes when she least expects it, it comes
to her that this anomie is freedom and not the chain

anchoring her to an old, dull self. The truth is in the hum
of her voice, its wrestling with chaste silence and pain

before her scream, the wild gutturals of her coaxing
him while he pants beneath her. It is in the wrenching dialect

of her desire, the way her sounds come like one choking
on holiness. In those moments of terrible abandon,

she feels like a true alien, a self outside herself,
free at last of something old and stern – the burden

of order and regret. Here, in this world she delves
into her hunger, not in search of truth, but for the wet

healing of a sprint through warm rain; not for memory
but for the history that glows in the future seductively.

END TIMES

Past midnight the surfeit of scriptures gluts
the television. The promise of simple answers,

the dogma of irrefutable truth, the sudden cuts
and giddy angles of well-suited, smooth preachers

are all she will watch. Outside, the wind
picks up. The earth is soft from rain and the green

of the repeating landscape – the way leaves spin
in the invisible light – belies the bloody schemes

of principalities and powers. The word
Armageddon returns to her dreams, the numerology

of the end times dancing before the flaming sword
of the Messiah. When she wakes she is holy

in the moonlight; her chest heaving, her eyes
dilating as if in dreams she has learned to fly.

SLIP

Adam
name her

couldn't
tame her

try to
hold her
close

but this world
too slippery for that

AFTERBIRTH

The raven himself is hoarse that croaks...
                                Lady Macbeth

A murder of crows noisily unsettles the sky.
Below, the muddy river folds against
its banks. The hot air reeks of a ripe sty

or an open grave. For Esther, who stains
the green coconut swamps with the speckled colour
of her fuchsia skirts and striped blouses that bloom

like wild gardenias in an unkind country, the odour
reminds her that the body is constantly decaying
(like the sharp pain of a womb rotting from

too much misuse) beneath the flesh. The hint
of the decay is in the distended, always warm
belly, and the blotched despair of slack skin.

Esther watches the crows, her eyes tearing
at these portents of loss and the body's rotting.

REDUX

The road slopes up – wet, it glows blue and white.

The moon will mad you when it catches in the crotch
of the mountain.
                        A woman is standing naked in the light.
We have been here before. A man, his face blotched
with green and silver, tries to will his mind to act,
to do something about this naked woman standing
on the road, her hair slick and soft. Her eyes make a pact
with his – so uncanny the way she turns his seeing
into a merciful blindness; this is a body lost to itself,
and her mind has slipped.
                                    You not from here?
he asks calmly. *I don't think so.*
                                    The air is deaf
to everything but their breathing. It has been a year
since that first time on the hill. This time she remembers
and her growing sorrow gives no shelter, drags them under.

LOSS

I cry last night
to see your face

grow soft
and slip away

even when you hold me
I know you gone.

RITUAL

At the edge of faith is fear, but ritual will guide us back
to the dumb comforts of belief. Stand beneath an acacia
tree and you will be falsely tented, caught in the tic-tac

netting of light, fading light – the soft dementia
of belief. Esther, in an askew cotton dress, sits
on a makeshift stool beneath a barren mango tree

and reads aloud from the *Book of Ruth*. She stops to rest
and dab her eyes when she feels the story
swell in her chest. These lessons come from dogged

memories. The reading followed by the daydream;
her dead lusts; her lover rising from the bog
to be dandy again, offering mango and cream.

It is the season of harvest, and a woman cries to hear
how love haunts, an addiction returning each living year.

DREAMING DELROY WILSON
To Wilson's version of Marley's "I'm Still Waiting"

The neighbours' bass seems to fall through the brittle shelter
of a giant tamarind tree; it steps with that slow patience
of ritual, and at once the sound seems to juice up the swelter

of the noon day. A man's voice weighs each line with dense
emotion, the phrasing a tightrope walk, each shuddering
stumble a performance. Esther falls into the sound as if

taken by a thick cloud. She is straining to see, remembering
the holes, grace notes and fatness in the song like a gift
held out – the whispered instructions of a pathfinder

whose language is an assurance despite the gloom ahead.
Said my feet, can't keep me up any more, and the crying
in his voice – the command of its confession is a red

door. She opens it, and is startled by the spinning
chaos, the answer to all things she fears. Delroy Wilson
is her guide, his voice crawls under her livid skin.

THE THINGS SHE KNOWS

Esther cannot admit that her thoughts at night are no longer
dreams but memories. She dares not confess that she has bought

Delroy Wilson's *Sarge*, placed it in the stereo so his tender
voice can take her through an avenue of broken houses, drought-

brittle yards, galvanized roofs and faces stoic as roughly
cut statues. The eyes are familiar, they speak a thick

stew of names; she is not a stranger. The heat is bloody
with a nation's memory, and Esther enters a closed-in shack

with mint leaves and crotons cluttering the grey concrete
floor, into the sound of a womb's throb and a mother's

damp, slippery cool hand smelling of onions. The heat
makes her arms, bosom, uneasy belly wet, and under

this hums the bass line, a one-drop and that dewy, sure voice
of a reggae man fulling her with rocksteady's fat noise.

AGE II

Grace says, *Esther, your eyes are clean*
as a new-day baby child.
Everything you see is green
every sound yellow and wild.

Grace weighs her breasts
like she would yams
pressing in to test
when they left the ground.

She says, *Your body is settled*
like fallow ground,
those breasts have suckled
a wayward generation;

you are the daughter
who would be my sister;
see how my sweater
covers you like water?

ESTHER'S NIGHTMARES

1. *The Accident*

A hollow house tucked into the shelter of fruit trees,
the neglect is barely showing – there is no life here.

Neighbours approach with averted eyes. They see
their own mortality in the narrative; the bare

windows, the silence. A family's disappearance,
the impossible efficiency of a tragedy that grows

with each telling: the man's body found by chance
by truant children diving in the river's slow

turn near the rocks; the two infants caught
like bloodied tabloid sheets in a tangled mess

of acacia bushes that grow below the rotted
edge of the roads; the tattered magenta dress

of the woman, have all been found. The car's carcass
rusts where river meets sea. We know the rest.

2. *The Drowning*

She struggles. Her dress ensnared in the submerged
roots of a mangrove tree, her arms flailing
until the red fabric rips; her body fights to emerge
into the cold blue night, after baptism, after shedding
her old skin.
           In this nightmare her man has high
cheekbones, damp, horse-eyes and something almost
like despair at the tedium of holding her tight,
firm, restraining her lashing body – so close
to him that she can't pull away before she grows
still, before she fills with river water, before
he is free of her, free to run to the bitch she knows
will hear that it was done quickly, painlessly.

He walks away not knowing that Esther will burst
into fresh air, naked, reborn and full of grace.

3. *The First Body*

In dreams she imagines a girl's slight body,
her ashy knees touching, her taut belly
a gentle bowl, her braids thick and knotty,
gentle on her shoulders. Her eyes glow
with recognition. She reaches upwards
and says, *Mama*, as if these are her first words.

Her calico dress is covered with thick cords
of green vines, obscenely red petals and a shower
of marigolds. Her arms are thin black twigs
and she holds herself as if she is afraid to feel
again, afraid to laugh. Above, the red sky promises
nothing but stories that will never heal.

Esther wakes with a stone deep in her belly
and the sadness of a soul missing its first body.

4.   *Esther's Daughter Returns*

She comes like an old quarrel, her face
red and fierce; her braids wild.
She is a child with too little grace;
then she says, *I hate to die.*

This is a dream. Awake, Esther
knows she can't fight
the resurrection of the terror
of forgotten truths. This light

is harsh, a knife-blade in the flesh,
and she can fight it back no more.
Monty is her peace, the lush
comfort that cradles her.

But Monty is fading into mist.
The ordinary is slipping into hope,
and uncertainty grows a fist
that ruins her peace. She gropes

for meaning, trying her hardest
to beat back the seepage of memory,
knowing that nothing but regret
will come with this resurrected body.

5. *Prognosis*

When a body surrenders to the truth of its decay,
when the calm truth-telling of a doctor offers
only months and the comfort of pills for the days

when the pain will be too much; the body prefers
forgetting and flight. A woman runs from the rotting
heart of her home, the room where she is waiting

for the cancer to begin to reek; she's sprinting
from the city, from memory, from knowing
herself, leaving the too early mourners, the plans

for the living that will survive her. She takes a bus
deep into a pitch-black night and then stands

dumbly in the hook of a chilly mountain road
dropping clothing, fear and every heavy load.

BACK OF MOUNT PEACE

Memory for her is the dumb back of a child,
her head shaded by a broad-brimmed straw
hat, the unfamiliar pattern of fabric against the wild

landscape, and so far in the distance a raw
walled house, something like a suggestion, a smudge
of yellow and red, some dark lines, the shape

of more reliable times. Memories are clouds lodged
in an unflappable sky where nothing escapes
the painter's final drying stroke. Memory for her

is the receding back of the child, growing
smaller, sinking into the tobacco green vapour –
a mist of loss, not sad, just a quiet haunting.

Memory for her is the faith that the girl will turn
full grown and whole, the way some memories can.

NEW SONG

On a morning silver as new galvanize,
Esther walks into a dew fall, her feet
glowing with wet, her voice a capsize
of petals on lush grass. There is heat

in her chest – the song comes in pockets
of regret and it is hard to move, her chest
full of air pressing against her breasts:
When my heart is overwhelmed, lead me...

Suddenly she sees through the mist
into the humid bowl of tongues dancing
and faces coming at her with answers. A fist
pounds the pulpit; she knows the stinging

of fear in her is a ritual, and the song
cuts her breath. She turns to the sun
to blind her until everything is gone –
a blank morning holding back the storm.

IN THE BEGINNING...

Monty Cupidon walks three miles
up the purple hills, deep into mist
each dusk, rain or shine. He smiles
when he reaches the flat crest

and looks over the valley to the sea
now golden and pink and soft,
and it is like prayer the way he
grows still. It is always enough.

So one day he finds in the dark
bend of the slicked-up road, under
a heavy *guinep* tree, the stark
naked body of a red woman, younger

than him, but bedlamized
in her eyes, turning, turning, her legs
covered with dead leaves; terrorized
by each tree crackle. He begs

softly till she grows calm,
lets him gather her in his coat
and slowly, promising no harm,
he leads her down to the soft coast.

EPILOGUE

COMFORT

Dearest Esther,

You said, *Find comfort in a damp wood's*
pink light and pure blue sky, the path sodden

with wet leaves, beyond the pale blood
of evening. Now my world has become

unlivable. You said *Find life in mountain air,*
smarting exposed flesh; don't bother

with the shelter of sweaters. This is purer.
We all go, you said, *leaving behind bewildered*

but resourceful people who will,
we know, cope, find paths in the woods, make

meaning of the tears, multiply what little
is left behind. I tried for your sake,

but I found no comfort in the woods, my love;
you have gone and no shelter is enough.

One love
Monty C

EXTRACTS FROM REVIEWS OF PREVIOUS COLLECTIONS

Progeny of Air
ISBN: 0 948833 68 8 £7.99

The book extends across a wide range of experiences, its first section focusing on incidents from childhood and adolescence. Many of these poems convey the painful cruelty of children, the pecking order of threat and coercion, terrible rites of passage. The playwright's skills of strong characterization are evident in the 'Hall of Fame', a series of vignettes of various characters, pupils and masters. The teachers are portrayed as figures of power and influence, but Dawes is aware of their off-duty lives too, striving to paint the whole picture. These portraits are invigorating and compassionate, suggesting that these men had futures as well as pasts, just like the boys on the threshold of adulthood. This is only one example of the way Dawes often offers a very different perspective on quite ordinary things, implying that time is more than simply a chronological device, and that culture and society is more than the hierarchy imposed upon 'the disorder of our terrible existence'. ... Dawes revels in the 'freedom to write the hidden'

He takes many admirable risks, borrowing narrative techniques from the storytelling tradition and rhythms from reggae. His vocabulary is a curious mixture of formal precise or prosaic words together with street slang and surprising compounds, all informed by a love of traditional 'English' poetry instilled at school in Jamaica - 'the jazz of words against words / making beauty in rhythm, sound, in twisted / clash of constructs we did not really grasp // but felt...'

I am grateful to Kwame Dawes for writing this book and bringing some heat to a grey and chilly autumn; grateful also to the Forward panel of judges for awarding it their First Collection Prize and so bringing it to the attention of a wider audience. Peepal Tree are bringing out two further books. I look forward to seeing what else this man can do.

Linda France *Poetry Review*

Prophets
ISBN: 0 948833 85 8 £7.99

Dawes fuses charisma and comment, imagination and documentary, invoking elements from the genre of popular culture, subculture, Jamaican ethos and song, effectively and lyrically. The aspects of lyricism and song are crucial to the carriage of the book's narrative. Song works in multiple ways – as praise, as penance, as pursuant of peace, as provider of pleasure. Song is also rhythm, and rhythm is reggae – indigenous, pure, full of bass resonance - which quietly provides not only a chorus leit-motif but also the syllabic markers that anchor the overall scale and story. Clarice and Thalbot who play the role of the protagonists of this arching operatic tale are dextrously cast.

Kwame Dawes' may elicit comparisons with 'novels-in-verse' or 'poems-as-narrative novel', especially with works such as Vikram Seth's *The Golden Gate*, Derek Walcott's *Omeros*, Craig Raine's *History: The Home Movie*, or even King James' version of The Bible. If comparisons have to be made, they ought to be done setting one thing absolutely clear, that here is one writer who writes out of his own tissue, with intelligence, originality, and passion, employing his very own idiom. If there are influences, then the most likely tints of the spectrum would include Walcott, Bob Marley, Christianity, colonialism, but all of these obliquely and indirectly. *Prophets* is a major book, a feast of spontaneity set in a serious framework. It is a narrative poem of sheer power, contemporaneity, and hope; one that is full of beauty, sadness, wisdom, and true humanism.

Sudeep Sen

Requiem
ISBN: 1 900715 07 4

Kwame Dawes' *Requiem* and *Jacko Jacobus* reveal a fresh talent, ready to take his place as one of the finest poets who has emerged during the 1990's. Like his two great compatriots, Derek Walcott and Kamau Brathwaite who, undoubtedly, represent the best tradition of Caribbean poetry, Dawes is similarly committed to capturing the essence of the Caribbean islands in expressions of compelling lyricism.

In *Requiem*, a work whose inspiration is derived from the illustrations of American artist, Tom Feeling's award-winning work, The Middle Passage: White Ships/Black Cargo, Dawes relies on the lyric form of the elegy to recreate the pain of suffering of slavery, and the possibility of redemption.

Indeed, in 'Requiem', the title poem, a lament for the many casualties of transatlantic slavery on the one hand and a celebration of hope on the other, the poet-persona reveals that he hears 'a blue note/ of lament, sweet requiem/for the countless dead,/ skanking feet among shell,/coral, rainbow adze,/webbed feet, making as if/to lift, soar, fly into new days'. In 'Vultures', the poet finds an apt metaphor for the beneficiaries - in the purely commercial sense - of the inhuman crime of slavery: 'These vultures speckle a blue sky/and learn the trade routes/ to the castles by the sea…' The gloom conveyed to the reader by the threnodic import of Dawes' imagery is remarkably tempered by a sense of hope, life, of survival, freedom: 'We sing laments so old, so true/then straighten our backs again.'

The technical accomplishment of Kwame Dawes' poetry is indicative of his ability to maintain a cool air while employing the genre of the lyric to explore his themes, and to cultivate an economy of expression while striving to maintain high quality in deployment of imagery.

Idowu Omoyele

Jacko Jacobus
ISBN: 1 900715 06 6

The Caribbean is finding a big new voice of alarm in Kwame Dawes. *Jacko Jacobus* is a long rollickingly control biographical-political-erotical epic – a novel in two-line verse-form almost – but always a poem – inspire by that most socially intriguing of Old Testament Bible 'prophets', the story of Jacob & Esau
Already I hear this on radio, on CD, see it in flim & video
Where nex to, Jacko

Kamau Brathwaite

Shook Foil
ISBN: 1 900715 14 7 £7.99

Few poets capture the mood of a generation. In *Shook Foil*, Kwame Dawes, 'drawing on inspiration as diverse as Derek Walcott, T. S. Eliot and Lorna Goodison,' attempts to define reggae and the major personality behind the success of the music, Bob Marley... who taught my generation how to be Jamaican and Pan-African (as if the two terms were mutually exclusive), how to honour ourselves and others, and finally how to love.

Throughout the collection, Dawes captures the many dimensions of reggae from the psalmic to the prophetic that are yet to be explored by other writers and musicians. Reggae remains unparalleled in its ability to absorb other influences and remain true to itself and to capture beauty, pain, and pleasure in a one-drop riddim. Its syncopation suggests a break, a gap – somewhere to fall with the faith that you will be caught – and this is what gives reggae its redemptive value. To really enjoy the music, you must believe. The same could be said of *Shook Foil*

Geoffrey Philp *The Caribbean Writer*

New and Selected Poems
ISBN: 1 900715 70 8 £9.99

In what seems a very short time, Kwame Dawes has established a reputation as a poet and critic of an unusually wide-ranging and sympathetic intelligence... One has a sense, reading over Dawes's work, that his is an active intelligence in the best tradition of the practitioner-critic, the different facets of his work – poetry, drama, public reading, reviewing, interviews with other Caribbean writers and academic criticism – each serving to inform his overall artistic project.

This is poetry dancing to a different drummer: the range of reference, the cultural assumptions bound into the poems, the cast and turn of the language, the lyrical drive... all of these announce another way of thinking about 'poetry in English', where both 'poetry' and 'English' are problematic terms to be challenged and redefined.

Stewart Brown *Poetry Review*

Impossible Flying
ISBN:9781845230395 £8.99

Kwame Dawes is one of the most important writers of his generation who has built a mighty and lasting body of work. *Impossible Flying* is surely his finest book of poetry thus far. These poems are both distilled and richly coloured. They synthesize rage, grief, pragmatism, and beauty into a love axis so deeply felt and powerfully expressed it startles.

– Elizabeth Alexander
Yale University

In *Impossible Flying*, Kwame Dawes brings Auden's dictum to mind: 'We must love one another or die.' Dawes confronts death, madness, grief and loss with the power of compassion, a fierce determination to honour his family and his beloved Jamaica. The poet's language is vivid and visceral; his courage and honesty blaze a path in poem after poem. This is the music of survival and transcendence. Indeed, the poetry of Kwame Dawes makes the impossible possible.

– Martín Espada

Majestic is the word that comes to mind reading the finely wrought poems of Kwame Dawes' *Impossible Flying*. Indeed, a sublime talent is needed to fashion poems of such capacious grace and energy. They are simultaneously intimate and political, intellectual and blood-filled, elegiac and enraptured: human in the most epic sense. No other poet of Dawes' generation is writing poems this relevant, this revelatory.

– Terrance Hayes

All Peepal Tree titles are available from our website: www.peepaltreepress.com; email hannah@peepaltreepress.com Or you can contact us at Peepal Tree Press, 17 Kings Avenue, Leeds LS6 1QS, UK (Tel +44 113 245 1703)